December And All That Follows

Andrea Pence

BookLeaf Publishing

Presentation by *BookLeaf Publishing*

Web: www.bookleafpub.com

E-mail: info@bookleafpub.com

ISBN: 9789357212823

First edition 2023

Dedicated to the memory of my parents, Shaun and Andy.

To my kids, Xander and Scarlette, who allow me to still catch glimpses in the magic of life.

Also to my clients - who give me purpose and a way to step outside of myself and help others.

PREFACE

Many of my clients are dealing with the complexities of grief as well as seasonal depression, as are so many people in the winter months. I have also had periods of struggle particularly after losing both of my parents very young. My mother passed away in 2013, and my father followed in early 2016. Even though I am very much grown, and have children of my own- it has presented a struggle at times when faced with the holidays, the cold months, and with getting older in general. This is about that, but this is also about hope, and different perspectives as you learn and grow. Ultimately it's just about letting emotions out and hopefully providing some kind of comfort because none of us are alone.

Silence

The depth of silence is endless.

Filled to the brim.
Calm.
Quiet.
Anticipation.
Sadness, and the ache that does not stop aching.
It will never stop aching.

Ever present, below the background noise.
Like a scene slightly outside of the frame
Oh! How we try to distract ourselves- Find a
way not to sink in.
Desperate attempt not to drown.
Fighting the waves to get through the days
But it is there.
Watching.
Waiting.
For the precise moment you are alone
Actually alone, not just the loneliness
A constant companion.
Vulnerable. Tired.
Nostalgic.
All the memories captured.
Kept prisoner.
Just out of reach.

The silence is the proof
The terrible heartbreaking evidence

…It is so incredibly loud.

2014

We called them “cookies”
Smug
Inexperienced
Young

“It won’t be a problem”
Because so far it hasn’t been.

Then one day it is.

It grows on you
And around you
Follows you like a shadow
Easy to lose focus when there’s only one focus
Enclosed room.
No windows.
No doors.

It’s okay, you don’t want to leave anyway.

Everyone is in the same boat
The only difference is the colors of the flags.
Weird bonds forged in necessity
Common understanding

I’ve never felt more accepted in my life.

No one wants to be sick.

It’s unavoidable.
It’s “part of it”

It’s one sickness or the other
Better with the blank thoughts
So that I can sit in my skin
Without wanting to rip myself apart.

Obsessed with forgetting
Can fix everyone’s life but my own
I’ve felt guilty my whole life anyway
With everyone dying
Honestly what’s the point?
No need to make it harder.

1 year becomes 2 years
…And 2 becomes 3
Living on coffee and cigarettes
Can’t be bothered to eat

Why prolong the inevitable if you’re already there?
Temptation.

Elation.
Relief and Despair.

Hurry up!
Turn the ship back!
The waves are too much this time!
…And you're nodding at the wheel

Eenie-Meeny-Miney-Mo

Not everyone will make it to tomorrow.

The Ghosts (Wishful Thinking)

Maybe we are the ghosts
Just like in that one movie
Completely oblivious
Making up inconveniences
While the time zips on cruelly.

Maybe somebody misses us too
The burden shifted elsewhere
Felt in different places
Different spaces
As we are simply unaware.

Life is for the living, they say
I have no doubt that's true
Although there must be some mistake if that doesn't include you.

So if there has to be this separation, maybe we're viewing it wrong.
A viewpoint born of desperation-
While the world keeps moving along.

Maybe we're the ghosts, because the pieces don't all fit.

Maybe we're stuck with the memories
...Of a scene that isn't lit.

Maybe we'll wake up tomorrow
From this crazy dream
And all will be well
We can then tell the tale
That nothing is quite what it seemed.

Black Stars and Satellites

I always knew deep down that you wouldn't
make it to being old.
You came with an unspoken expiration date.

I think I knew it almost from the start -
But the terrifying thing there
Is how alike we were.

If I ever had a lost twin
You were it
But dealing with myself was exhausting
Like a magnet at times
Like a fire at others

It burned me
Over and over.

We communicated through music
Through lyrics, and vague statements
But I understood.
All too much.

And on the day that music died
Our trains had fully crashed into each other.
...For the last time, this time...

I had finally met you on your own terms.

Recipe for disaster.

Blaze of glory.

...I wouldn't see you again.

You sent me a message 2 days before you died
I didn't get it until you were dead.
This is the first time I've told anyone that.
I wouldn't have responded anyway.
...But sometimes it still bothers me.

And I wonder what you meant
Because, for once, the meaning of the song
eluded me.

Sometimes I worry that I figured it out.
The last mystery.
Maybe not so much of a mystery at all.

What's a fitting end to a story that would
NEVER have a happy ending?

Is this it?

20 years of history

And oh! What a ride it was.

It didn't change the fact that
I always knew I'd say goodbye to you
Before it was time
Felt it in my very being.

Still only managed to jump off at the last
possible stop.

The Uncatchable Criminal

Time is the greatest thief
Never punished
Allowed to keep running rampant
Destroying everything it encounters.

Time is a predator
Stalking its prey
Creeping up behind even the best souls

It loves catching everyone by surprise
...And then running out.

You can try to stop it
Efforts in futility
Ticking
Ticking
Ticking.

Not that much different from a beating heart
But when you put them against each other in battle
...There's only one who can ever win.

Time is a liar
A cunning narcissist

Manipulating you into letting your guard down
Pretending to move slowly
False sense of security
And no matter how much I tell you

You'll still never see it coming.

Burn This Letter

You didn't think your life would turn out how it
did.
You said as much
In a letter
One you told me to burn
…I don't remember if I did, or not.
I'm sorry.
I've lost so many things along the way
For better or for worse.

Echoes from 20 years ago
How has it been that long?
All 20 years gave you was a voice that no longer
speaks
Except in my head
For better or for worse

I can't say I was much in the way of a
confidante
I didn't understand the sadness then
The helplessness fate brings
That's something you gain with time
With experience
For better or for worse.

I can see you now through a different lens
More sympathetic, more empathetic
Trying to put puzzle pieces together
Like we all are

...Only for something to keep sweeping them away...

Trying to make sense of the cards dealt
What an odd game of chance
I have played a similar hand
For better or for worse.

We want to do the best we can
It will always feel that we fall short
Even if we don't
Blind spot in the mirror
We try, we try
You and I
For better or for worse.

I wish I could have understood you more then
Because I never will now
Wish I had asked the questions
While you were still around.

I don't think we're as different as I originally thought
Both of us struggled

Both of us fought
For better or for worse.

Irrelevant

I exist in the background
If I exist at all

An afterthought
Not worth mentioning
Walking a tightrope
Until the fall.

Then everyone wants to stare.
Everyone wants to talk.

My fault
As always

The problem noone tries to solve.

I've heard people say they're the "background friend"
But I'm in the background
No matter what situation I'm in.

That's how it's been
As long as I can remember
A tree no one sees
Until someone shouts "Timber!"

Always guilty for being a bother
Terrified to inconvenience
Feeling anxiety
Fawning
When things cannot be seamless.

Everyone matters

Except for me

I guess that's the way it has to be.

The Maze in Your Head

When the world ended
It was 2012

But we all woke up the next day.

Things started changing after that
After we were moved
Steady streams of consciousness
Trapped, as we were
Pretending to evolve
Gaslit
By memories that didn't seem quite right.

We kept marching
Ants to a hill
Lambs to the slaughter

It's our nature, after all
Our construct
Familiar is what we want
Even if that means shutting our eyes.

Ignorance is bliss.

Computer programs
Semblance of life
The sadness cloaked over
Decorated with a bow

Too busy in our imagined lives to see
Too eager to accept the explanations
Writing on the wall
...But we forgot how to read on purpose.

Many moves by now
Consciousness like scrambled eggs
It's a whole different thing we're becoming
No wonder everyone's sick.

We jumped the shark
As a species, as a whole
There's no turning back
But the tv won't tell you that.

Do you remember at all who you used to be?
Made of broken parts
It resembles just enough
To keep the uncanny valley effect at bay.

Deep down
You know
You'll never be home again.

The religious preach of a paradise
Beautiful
Gold paved

Unaware the rapture happened

...And there was no one worth being saved.

Reds and Greens

Reds and greens and all the noise
All the comfort, all the joy.

It's like a moment hasn't passed
Despite the fact that nothing lasts.

It all feels familiar
The smells and the sounds
Despite the fact the same people aren't around.

We make it through, like we're supposed to do
While the calendar marches on.

Reds and Greens and all the noise
Santa will come for the girls and the boys
The tree will be lit, stockings hung by the fire
Decorations and lights, for you to admire.

We try to pretend that it feels like home
That we do not feel so alone
Depression just doesn't go with the tone
It's a happy time of year.

There's always the sense something's just not
quite "right"

That the silence is eerie
Even for a silent night
Haunted by the memories of those lost from our sight
Reds and greens
Everywhere
Shining ever so bright.

Something in the Air

The wind
It blows
The past right in.

For only a minute
The scenery shifts

Hypnotic
Time travel
The door swinging wide
You can't help but notice the darkness outside.

Broken streetlights
Calling us back home…

The Elephant Man

Never been a fan
Of talking
Just to talk

Self important
"Know it alls"
They never "walk the walk"

Egos running rampant
Chattering incessantly
To be the center
The focal point
"Look at me!"
"Look at me!"

Never been a fan
Of the ones who are "always right"
Trampling on others
Determined just to fight

Not for the greater good
No, it's never that
Only some semblance of being ahead
When in reality, they're last

The loudest in a room
Usually has no clue
And makes themselves a jackass
While insisting they speak truths

Kings of nowhere
Leaders of none
Control and intimidation
Their idea of fun

I've just never been a fan of those who view themselves "above"
Narcissism incarnate
No empathy
No love.

Amassing an army of "excusers"
So no one can call them out as abusers

All the worlds a show, you see
But the actors are really good
Most of the time you never see it's a wolf inside the hood

Only concerned with getting their way
No matter what the cost
They lay some very clever traps

…And so many lives are lost…

Que Sera, Sera

Blank pages
Worn at the edges
As if someone read them before

Names
Dates
On display

People who'll wonder briefly
And then move on
Dedication of time
Replaced
But never the same

A story unfinished
The never-ending
End
Unexpected and abrupt

No preparation
So much space to write

Alas-
No one knows where the words go
Or how to arrange them

Draw a picture instead
A heart
A heartbreak

Crushed under the weight of unknowns
That which is unspoken
For eternity to be as such

What will be, will be
And what won't
Is unchanging
The sky is indifferent
No matter the tears.

The Intruders Are Already Inside

"The end is near"
The sign says
"It's been over"
I say
To no one in particular
Except myself.

Me
Who doesn't listen
Even to own voice.

Me
Who is constantly trying to drown it out.

It's all got to be a certain way
It's anyone's guess what THAT is
Don't ask me
Blind leading the blind.

Melancholy
What's new
The end is just another beginning.

Beginnings
We LOVE those
Desperately throw hope at it
Like feeding a wild animal
Then being mad when it attacks you.

Same thing over and over
We just don't learn.

All that we destroy was once worth something
As always
We just thought we mattered more.

The Void That Came From Ashes

I belong to somewhere
That no longer exists
I'm not sure anymore
If it did

It's possible I belong nowhere
False memories
To cushion that blow.

We all want to belong
Though, we never feel like we do

Lead by breadcrumbs
Worn pathways
That don't look like you remember
The shadow too tall

It doesn't feel the same
Can't quite point out why
Something amiss
Can't help but feel
That it's you.

"I belong here!" you scream
As if to prove it
Alas-
Only the years answer back.

The Story (X and S)

I wonder what your perception will be
When you look back on the years
How will you see me,
When you gaze in the rear view mirror?

You'll be my judge and my jury
In a court I'll never see
You will be the only opinion that matters
When it comes to the story of you, and me

When one day I'm gone
As is the cycle
What bits of me will you carry on?
What parts of me, are recycled?

I only hope who I was
To you
Doesn't leave any doubts

That I mostly left you "with"
And rarely left you "without"

I'll be long gone by the time you truly see me
As a person

And not a figure
Trying to do my best
For the sake of something bigger.

Know that I could only be proud
Of you,
And who you're destined to be
Know that you're the best things
That ever came from me.

You've always been the stars in my sky
I hope you know it's true
I hope you know I tried my best

In the story of me, and you.

Beyond Our Sight

My ears
Always listening

Catch in my chest
Lump in my throat.

On edge,
Waiting for disaster
Only a moment away.

Mind creating scenarios
That I've seen before in tv shows
Fighting the urge
To hide.

Nightmares constructed
With every car passing
Every dog barking
Every footstep that sounds angry

Overactive imagination
Survival instinct
Never can tell the difference.

Can’t let the guard down
Because the one time you do
You might be sorry.

“Might” is a dangerous word
Though it pales in comparison
To “humans”

Humans will always embody chaos
They are the biggest danger of all.

Still

Traffic quiet
Can hear a pin drop

Everyone is already where they're supposed to be
Except the ones that no longer have a choice.

They sit still
Eternally
Whether rain or shine

Do they know it's Christmas?

I don't know if "yes" or "no" is better.

Watching us like a movie
One they were supposed to be in
Scenes cut short

The empty chair
Missing present
A part of everything,
Even the conversation
Lingering silences
Unable to chime in
Still so much left to say.

Christmas has a certain magic to it
A feeling that miracles could happen
If you just believe enough

But,
Not every wish can come true.

The Highway

Youth is
Temporary

Symptoms of naivete
Feelings of immortality
For you
And all those you love

No end in sight
Rolling down a seemingly endless road

The bumps are slight
At first
Minor inconvenience
Barely noticeable
Especially as sure as you are

A fantastic mirage
The ego
Beautiful denial
Ignorance
Like Bliss
Fleeting
…It never lasts long enough…

A few days later
You wonder
"Why are there so many potholes lately?"
"What's wrong with my car?"

You wait
Patiently
For the pathway to clear

Downed power lines
Blocking the way through.

The next day,
You grow confused
When you notice the road signs disappeared
Along with the exits
Not as many tail lights ahead in the distance
Just yesterday
A sea of lights

Suddenly you become aware
For the first time

No U-Turns are possible.

You are traveling irreversibly
On a one way road.

The Avalanche of Identity

Space between
Wrong and right
Thin margins
Intruding into each others dialogue

We will never be one or the other

…That won't stop someone else from slapping on a label…

The sum of us
Romanticized
Or
Demonized

No video to watch back
Pieces of memories

We don't consider
The brain changes them…

Each time we remember something
A tiny bit different.

Snowball rolling down the hill.

We just want to hold onto the pieces
What our foundation is comprised of
Like a crackhead checking his pocket
Over
And
Over
To make sure all isn't lost.

Can't hold onto the intangible
Constructed by flawed logic

Our ego makes us insist.

We don't even know we're lying.

The Christmas Episode

It's not cold enough for December
It lacks the right design
Rain is not the same as snow
Something's clearly misaligned.

It's not cheery enough for a holiday
Guess we'll have to just make due
It's not silent enough for a silent night
The mistletoes crooked too.

The lights don't shine as bright as they did
The air is not as clear
Funny how your opinions change
When you're no longer a kid.

Still, there's something calming
Despite all that is not
Something soothing about the evening
That leaves you less distraught.

Make a few adjustments
Don't cry and miss your cue
Little eyes are watching
Childlike wonder still brand new.

The Homecoming

You go through the rest of your life
Expecting to see them
Anticipating reconnection
A feeling deep in your bones

Your mind never puts it together
No matter how long
They won't be home for Christmas
But, your heart wants that to be wrong.

You know the facts of the matter
Yet struggle to accept
Forever is a really long time
Way out of your usual depth.

It doesn't seem possible
As the years continue to dredge on
Feels like you were with them just yesterday
They can't really be gone.

Hits you out of nowhere
A page turned in an endless book
Tired of reading the same thing
Mocking you every time you look.

We try to keep the faith
'Cause we really have no choice
That one day we'll meet again
And finally hear their voice.

Forever and its grasp
Now a thing of the past
A new forever emerging
One that will truly last.

www.ingramcontent.com/pod-product-compliance
Lightning Source LLC
Chambersburg PA
CBHW051739130826
49812CB00033B/923
9789357212823